For People in Love

FOR PEOPLE IN LOVE

Romantic Thoughts by Pearl S. Buck,
Sara Teasdale, the Duke of Windsor,
Paul Engle, William Carlos Williams,
May Swenson and Many Others

Edited by Tina Hacker

HALLMARK EDITIONS

Designed by Lilian Weytjens.

The publisher wishes to thank those who have given their kind permission to reprint material included in this book. Every effort has been made to give proper acknowledgments. Any omissions or errors are deeply regretted, and the publisher, upon notification, will be pleased to make necessary corrections in subsequent editions.

ACKNOWLEDGMENTS: "The Quest" from *Words of Love* by Pearl S. Buck. Copyright © 1974 by Creativity, Inc. Reprinted with permission of The John Day Company, publisher, and Harold Ober Associates, Inc. "30 Cents, Two Transfers, Love" excerpted from *Rommel Drives on Deep Into Egypt* by Richard Brautigan. Copyright © 1970 by Richard Brautigan. Reprinted by permission of Delacorte Press/Seymour Lawrence and Helen Brann Agency. "Rondo" from *Selected Poems of Alfred Kreymborg, 1912-1944*, by Alfred Kreymborg. Copyright © 1945 by Alfred Kreymborg; renewal © 1973, Dorothy Kreymborg. Reprinted by permission of the publishers, E. P. Dutton & Co., Inc. "Miracle" by Mark Davidson reprinted by permission from the March 1976 issue of *Good Housekeeping Magazine*. © 1976 by the Hearst Corporation. "Discovery" by Grace I. Knoles reprinted by permission from the May 1976 issue of *Good Housekeeping Magazine*. © 1976 by the Hearst Corporation. Excerpt from an article by Helen Worden, quoting the Duke of Windsor, reprinted by permission of the Liberty Library Corporation. Copyright 1937 Macfadden Publications, Inc. "Swifter Than These" reprinted with permission of Macmillan Publishing Co., Inc. from *Country Poems* by Elizabeth Coatsworth. Copyright 1931, 1933, 1934, 1935, 1936, 1938, 1942 by Elizabeth Coatsworth Beston. "Faults" reprinted with permission of Macmillan Publishing Co., Inc. from *Collected Poems* by Sara Teasdale. Copyright 1917 by Macmillan Publishing Co., Inc. Renewed 1945 by Mamie T. Wheless. "Epitaph" by William Carlos Williams, from *Collected Earlier Poems*. Copyright 1938 by New Directions Publishing Corporation. Reprinted by permission of New Directions Publishing Corporation. "She Touched Me" from *I Love to Have You Touch Me* by Dick Sutphen. © 1971 by Dick Sutphen. Published by Valley of the Sun Publishing Company. Reprinted with permission. "Love Is" from *To Mix With Time* by May Swenson. Copyright © 1963 by May Swenson. Used by permission of the author. "Lovesong" by Frances Higginson Savage is reprinted by permission of the author and *The Lyric*. "Under a Full Moon" by Katherine Edelman is reprinted by permission of the author and *The New York Times*. "The Lovers" by Dena Reed is reprinted by permission of the author. Illustrations on pages 20 and 30 reprinted by permission of Liberty Library Corporation.

© 1977, Hallmark Cards, Inc., Kansas City, Missouri.
Printed in the United States of America. Standard Book Number: 87529-523-1.

FOR PEOPLE
IN LOVE

THE WORLD OF LOVE

Love creates its own world,
sets its own pace —
        now rushing swiftly
                toward new discoveries,
        now pausing to savor
                some quiet joy,
tenderly guarding
        each golden moment…
warmly embracing
        each glorious day.

AMY CASSIDY

MIRACLE

A miracle is the swoop of a bird
And the gesture of your hand.
A miracle is the blaze of the sun
And the sparkle of your eyes.
A miracle is the crash of the waves
And the flute of your voice.
A miracle is the cool of the wind
And the warm of your arms.
A miracle is rain and roses
And all else in creation
When I'm
With you.

MARK DAVIDSON

*L*ove's sweet music
opens
hard rock drummin
really hummin
comin on strong
builds
ascending
crescending
sending vibrations
quickly gone
mellows
gaining beauty
sustaining harmony
refraining gently
on and on and on.

STEPHEN FINKEN

30 Cents, Two Transfers, Love

Thinking hard about you
I got onto the bus
and paid 30 cents car fare
and asked the driver for
    two transfers
before discovering that I
    was alone.

Richard Brautigan

Kissing
and
Making up
is
almost worth
getting into
a fight over!

ANNE PARKER

RONDO

Even you

are variations,

variations

never the same:

Hair and eyes and

mouth and moods and

curves and kisses —

Girl, woman,

mother, child,

each and all so

never the same.

So many to keep!

So many to come!

ALFRED KREYMBORG

THE LITTLE THINGS

In spite of tubes of toothpaste
    that he squeezes in the middle,
And the damp and dainty lingerie
    she strings across the tub;
In spite of his one hundredth telling
    of the same old riddle,
And her volunteering every week
    to host her Handcrafts Club;
In spite of all the gadgets for his car
    he's always buying,
And her endless diet dinners
    when she wants to lose an ounce;
In spite of all those "little things"
    that sometimes seem so trying,
The way they love each other
    is all that really counts!

Richie Tankersley

LOVE...   Discovers
                  reaches
                        touches
                              holds...
            cares
                  comforts
                        warms
                              enfolds...
            listens
                  speaks
                        gives
                              receives...
            knows
                  seeks
                        trusts
                              believes...
            laughs
                  cries
                        reassures...
            hopes
                  desires
                        and endures.

                              BARBARA LOOTS

*L*ove will teach us all things:
but we must learn how to win love;
it is got with difficulty:
it is a possession dearly bought
with much labor and in long time;
for one must love not sometimes only,
for a passing moment, but always.

FYODOR DOSTOEVSKY

LOVESONG

My love is like a cool wind
across a parching plain;
my love is like a larkspur cloud
that brings you longed-for rain.

My love is like a leafy elm
amid a summer meadow,
lifting a wide green parasol
woven of sun and shadow.

It is a ceaseless lyric stream
from which to drink your fill,
its changeful currents running clear
and fresh and bountiful.

It is an eager leaping flame
that feeds upon desire,
a constant candle in the dark,
a hospitable fire.

It is a roof to shelter you,
a cloak against the gale,
a song to cheer and comfort you,
and it will never fail.

Frances Higginson Savage

OUR FIRST DATE

The movie — dull,
the film broke twice,
the popcorn — stale,
they had no ice.

The drive-in — crowded,
the burgers — burnt,
the ice cream — warm,
the french fries weren't.

The car broke down,
we got home late,
you took my hand —
the night was great!

KARL LAWRENCE

FAULTS

They came to tell your faults to me,
They named them over one by one;
I laughed aloud when they were done,
I knew them all so well before —
Oh, they were blind, too blind to see
Your faults had made me love you more.

SARA TEASDALE

DISCOVERY

In silence I have often stood alone
Upon this hill, and felt the warm romance
Of summer skies, or watched the silver glance
Of wings in moonlight, till a scene long known
Became a haunt of mystery, each stone
Revealed a polished floor for fairies' dance.
It seemed a nightingale could not enhance
A world with flowers of moonlight overgrown.
And so I thought, and even dreamed I knew
The language of the trees, the hilltop's lore,
And felt possessed of all that I could view,
Enriched with that I could not wish were more;
But breathlessly I stand tonight with you,
And know that I have never seen before.

Grace I. Knoles

UNDER A FULL MOON

The moon is full: I stand within the tide
Of silver falling from the distant sky,
Of some strange force vibrating through the night;
The fields around reach out in bridal white;
The air holds almost sounding of a cry.
No roof is passed; no meanest trail is left
Bare of adorning beauty; none bereft;
The world before my eyes is silver-dyed...
Tonight I almost hear the faint, far word
That Romeo whispered, lovely Juliet heard.

Katherine Edelman

An old willow

    with hollow branches

    slowly swayed

his few high bright tendrils

    and sang:

Love is a young green willow

    shimmering at the bare wood's edge.

WILLIAM CARLOS WILLIAMS

WHEN LOVE ARRIVES

I waited for someone
to play me soft music,
waited for someone
to write me sweet rhyme,
waited for someone
to bring me bright flowers,
waited for someone
to love me sometime.
Then he came along,
and my heart started singing
as I read the poetry
of his warm smile,
he brought me the beautiful brightness
of sharing,
and I knew I'd been waiting
for him all the while.

KAREN RAVN

I f I could fly I would soar into the clouds
and sculpture one in your image!
Then, all eyes could see your beauty.

ARTHUR BOZE

Words alone cannot tell you of my love,
for even a silence when we're together
is filled with unheard music.

CECIL LONG

Sand Writers

Seeking crumbs of immortality,
They write their names on sand
In lightsome love;
The sun shrugs their small labors,
And the moon
Will spur its tides
To the inevitable erasure;
Still, for the hour, they, the innocents,
Savor each other,
Dare the sea and Time to chip
One iota
From discovered selves.

They <u>were</u> here today.
In truth what lifetime
Measures more?

BESSIE F. COLLINS

THE QUEST

Love is a questing spirit,
Seeking where to find
A human frame to live in,
A human heart to bind.

A human heart to bind, dear love,
And so I offer mine.
Accept this heart and, if you will,
Use it as bread and wine.

PEARL S. BUCK

LOVE BELONGS TO LOVERS

Love is more than common interests, shared
experiences, similar backgrounds. It goes
beyond a handsome smile or a cute way. It is the
inexplicable, often irrational, connection that is
made between two people.

Poets can merely describe its moods.
Psychologists can only comment on its obvious
aspects. Historians can do no more than trace
its markings in the sands of time.

Love belongs to lovers. Two people who share
what is deepest in their hearts. Never completely
understanding it, yet never doubting its reality.

Paul M. Albe

THE LOVERS

Her hands drip tenderness
And, oh, his voice
Is kind as a caress.
Their eyes rejoice
And cling and speak each secret thing
With rapture.

Flaming fountains play
Within them, and a flood
Of fire and music mingles in their blood.
Who would capture Beauty for a day,
Must love!
There is no other way.

DENA REED

MEETING

Here in the crowded

City street

Hundreds and thousands

Watch us meet.

We walk around

Square, circle, loop.

Crowd is alone.

We are a group.

PAUL ENGLE

LOVE IS a rain of diamonds
in the mind

the soul's fruit
sliced in two

a dark spring
loosed at the lips of light

under-earth waters
unlocked from their lurking
to sparkle in a crevice
parted by the sun

a temple
not of stone but cloud
beyond the heart's roar
and all violence

outside the anvil-stunned domain
unfrenzied space

between the grains of change
blue permanence

one short step
to the good ground

the bite into bread again

MAY SWENSON

GOD BLESS ALEXANDER GRAHAM BELL!

God bless Alexander Graham Bell!
I hope that he's in heaven smiling now
with the knowledge
that his brainchild
spanned a continent tonight,
bringing the words I needed…
"Please hurry home!"
   "I'll meet you at the airport!"
      "I love you
          very much!"

DEAN WALLEY

S o long as you know

she loves you,

don't ask her what she means by love.

If she asked you, you couldn't tell;

or if you could tell, your romance would

probably come to an end....

THE DUKE OF WINDSOR

A SINGLE MIND

So close we two have grown,
it seems
we have become
a single mind.
He knows my words
before I speak,
so closely
are our thoughts entwined.
So very deep
our love has grown,
he understands
each look and sigh.
And sometimes,
magically,
it seems
that he is more myself
than I.

BARBARA BURROW

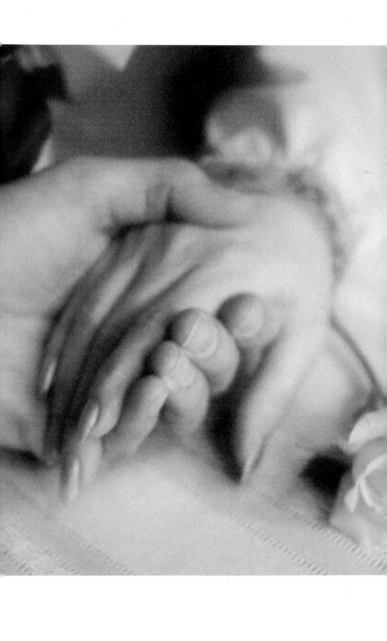

WAITING FOR HER

I like to be waiting for her, to be standing at the corner watching people go by and knowing I'm luckier and happier than every one of them.

I always get there early, not wanting to miss a single moment with her. The time passes quickly, with sweet rememberings of laughter, little gestures of love, something she said just that morning to make me smile.

I feel a sudden joy when I first see her approaching, getting closer, almost here — that first look that says "I love you."

I like to be waiting for her, to be anticipating the most wonderful thing that can happen to my day.

Hadin Marshall

Swifter Than These

Swift comes the summer,
Swift is the rose,
And swiftly the river
Seaward flows,
Swift the bird's wing,
And the skimming stone,
And swiftly the heart
May know its own.

Swift is the vessel,
And swift the wave,
And the fish that darts
Through its coral cave,
Swift is the wind
Blowing over the seas,
But a heart may be swifter
Even than these!

ELIZABETH COATSWORTH

I SEARCH FOR WORDS

I search for words to fashion into speech
The form and substance of our love; as well
Try to define a mountain's lofty reach
Or ocean's crashing sound within a shell.
One cannot capture sunlight's dappled sheen
Or spiraling and rush of swallow's wings;
And who can tell of meadows, gold and green,
Or prison earth's majestic, lovely things?
No words, however eloquent, convey
The radiance that shimmers in a star,
Nor sound the depth of beauty before day
Or tell the sweet enchantment where you are.
I search for words, but none can quite reveal
The depth and beauty of the love we feel.

Katherine Nelson Davis

MEANT FOR EACH OTHER

Though I prefer
    to lounge about
        while he is on the go,
And I crave
    chocolate ripple
        and he likes pistachio,
Though I would choose
    a foreign film
        and he'd go see John Wayne,
And I'd select
    a posh hotel
        while he'd camp in the rain,
Though each of us
    has different tastes,
        on one thing we agree—
The kind of love we share
    suits us perfectly!

NAN ROLOFF

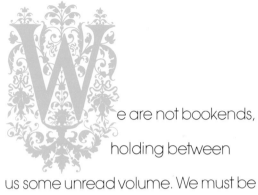

e are not bookends,

holding between

us some unread volume. We must be

authors, combining our styles to write

new chapters in the book of love.

GEORGE WEBSTER DOUGLAS

SHE TOUCHED ME

She touched me
and I reacted
in vibrations
of warm colors —

and the
search lights
of my soul
scanned the
night sky
to announce
the grand opening
of my mind.

DICK SUTPHEN

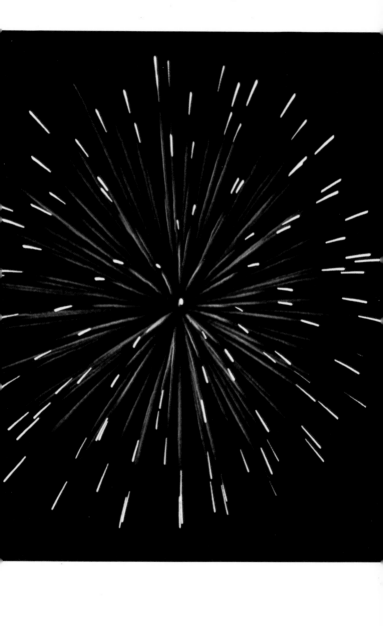